Zachary Zormer Shape Transformer

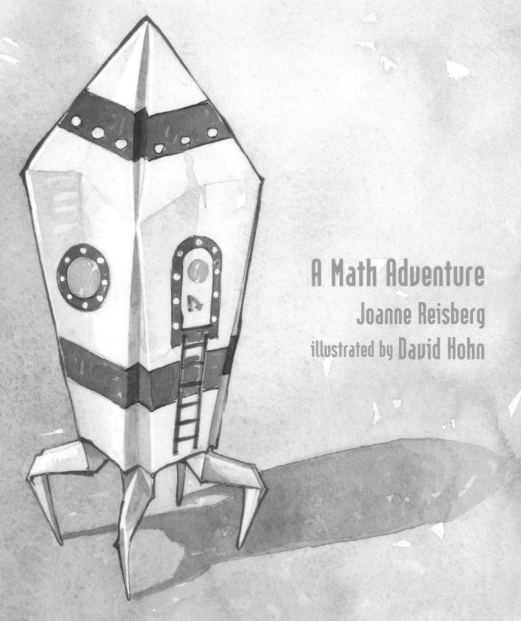

A Math Adventure

Joanne Reisberg

illustrated by David Hohn

Charlesbridge

*To my grandchildren Sam and Tori Reisberg, Meredith and Lars-Gunnard Johnson
And my grandnephew and nieces Alex, Merdena, and Lara Freeburg — J.R.*

To Heidi Lindner's entire 4th grade class — D.H.

Text copyright ©2006 by Joanne Reisberg
Illustrations copyright ©2006 by David Hohn
All rights reserved, including the right of reproduction in whole or in part in any form.
Charlesbridge and colophon are registered trademarks of Charlesbridge Publishing, Inc.

Published by Charlesbridge, 85 Main Street, Watertown, MA 02472
(617) 926-0329 • www.charlesbridge.com

Library of Congress Cataloging-in-Publication Data
Reisberg, Joanne A.
  Zachary Zormer : shape transformer : a math adventure / by Joanne
Reisberg ; illustrated by David Hohn.
     p. cm.
  ISBN-13: 978-1-57091-875-9; ISBN-10: 1-57091-875-9 (reinforced for library use)
  ISBN-13: 978-1-57091-876-6; ISBN-10: 1-57091-876-7 (softcover)
  1. Shapes--Juvenile literature. I. Hohn, David, 1974- ill. II. Title.
  QA445.5.R457 2006
  516'.15--dc22
                              2005020749

Printed in Korea
(hc) 10 9 8 7 6 5 4 3 2 1   (sc) 10 9 8 7 6 5 4 3 2 1

It was Friday, Zachary Zormer's favorite day of the week. He looked around. "Oh rats, I forgot! I was supposed to bring in something fun to measure!" Zack sank down in his chair. "Maybe Ms. Merkle won't call on me."

Tyler marched up to the front of the room and held up a photograph. "My mom and I raised this orchid," he bragged. "It grew a flower that was eight inches wide and got first place at the state fair. We won the blue ribbon and my picture was on the front page of the newspaper."

For Friday:
Bring in somethin
interesting to
measure.

As Tyler strutted back to his seat, all the kids leaned over to see the photograph up close.

Zack slumped down further. "I can't even grow mold on an old sandwich," he groaned.

"Yes, Zack?" Ms. Merkle asked. "Do you want to go next?"

What? He hadn't meant to say anything!

Zack shoved his hands into his pockets as he walked to the front of the room.

He felt a dime, a pencil stub, and a folded-up piece of paper he had meant to throw in the recycle bin.

He turned to face the class.

Everyone was looking at him.

"I got it!" he said aloud.

Zack pulled the paper out of his pocket and unfolded it. Then, he tore off one end. "This paper strip is only eight and a half inches long, but I can make it double its length." He twisted one end of the strip then taped the ends together. "Now it's seventeen inches!"

The kids were used to Zack's jokes. "Yeah, right." "What planet do you live on?" "No way."

7

"I'll prove it to you," Zack said. "I'll draw a line down the center without lifting the marker. When I'm done the line will be on both sides of the paper, and it will be 17 inches long."

All the kids leaned forward to watch.

"In a space station, where there's no gravity, I could make an exercise track shaped like this," Zack said. "That way astronauts could run twice as far."

The kids couldn't believe their eyes. Ms. Merkle told the class that the loop is called a Moebius Strip. All around the room, kids began making their own one-sided loops.

Zack sat down grinning. He thought to himself, "That was close. Next time I'll remember to bring something in." At the back of the room, Tyler was scowling.

Before long it was Friday again. This time Zack was ready. At least, he thought he was. "Rats, where is it?" He searched all of the pockets in his backpack. He even turned the pack upside-down and shook it. His picture frame was gone.

For Friday:
Bring in a rectangle and tell us how you found its perimeter.

Tyler waved his hand frantically in the air. He wanted to go first.

"My uncle climbed the highest mountain in the world and found this 400 million-year-old fossil. Its perimeter is only 6 inches, but this little seashell fossil proves that the mountains were once under the sea! My uncle was going to give it to a museum, but he let me keep it."

"Wow!" said Zack. "The oldest thing I have is the banana at the bottom of my locker."

As Tyler walked back to his seat, he announced, "I think Zack has something really interesting to show next."

"Zachary?" Ms. Merkle asked.

The color drained from Zack's face. He had nothing – and Tyler knew it.

Zack slowly got to his feet and took a deep breath. In his pockets he found an oval rock, an empty gum wrapper, and a crumpled-up hall pass. He'd lost his picture frame, but he had an idea.

In front of the class, Zack pulled out the hall pass and smoothed it out. "This is a small piece of paper," he said. "It's about 4 inches long and 6 inches wide, so it has a perimeter of about 20 inches," he paused, "but I can make it big enough to walk through."

Tyler laughed loudly, but everyone else looked curious.

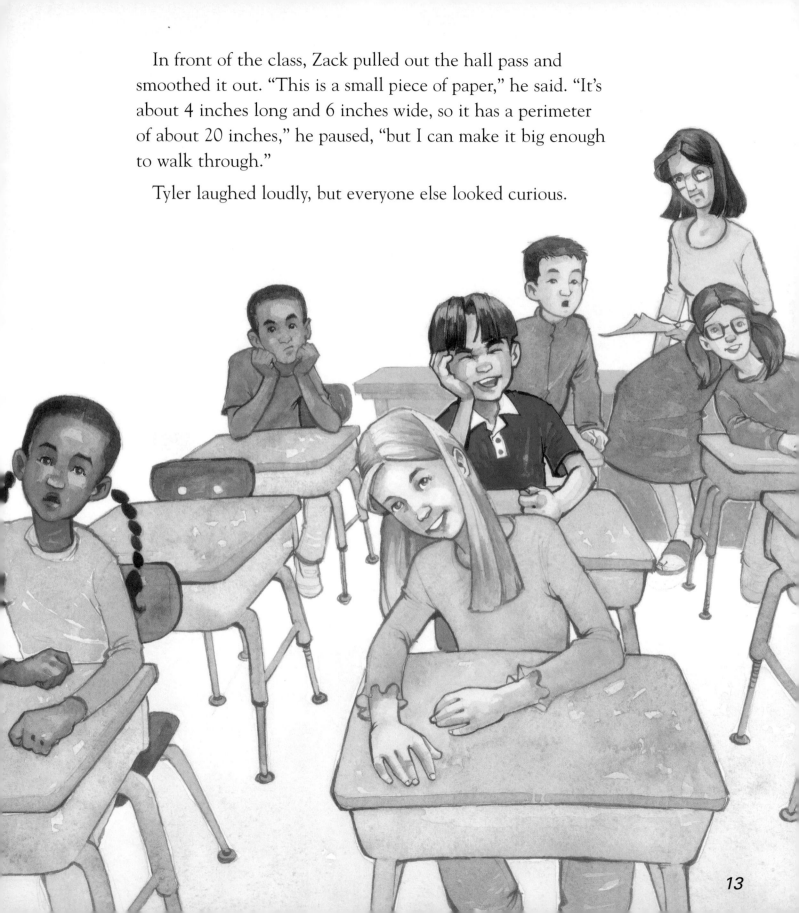

Zack picked up a pair of scissors. "I just have to fold the paper and make some cuts." When he put the scissors down, he shook the paper and it became a big, zigzagging frame. Zack pulled the frame down over his head.

"The amount of paper is still the same but now the edges are almost five times longer," he explained. "This is important because when I'm building a space station, I'll need to make the most of every material."

The kids were silent at first. Then they started clapping! Everyone took out scissors and paper and began to cut. Everyone but Tyler.

Before Zack knew it, it was Friday again.

It was raining hard so his dad drove him to school. They got there only minutes before the bell. Zack jumped out of the car and raced up the front steps. "Made it!" he shouted.

Then he realized he'd left his backpack in the car.

When Zack sloshed into the classroom, Ms. Merkle said, "Wonderful—we have perfect attendance today."

Perfect attendance! What was he thinking? He could have stayed home in bed with a fever, a nosebleed, or a weird jungle disease. He muttered, "Maybe Friday isn't my favorite day anymore."

One by one, kids told about the area of a notebook, a library card, a CD case, and so on. Soon only Tyler and Zack were left. When Tyler was called, he swaggered to the front of the room.

"My grandfather always says, 'Good things come in little packages.' This little bar means a lot to him, even though its area is only one square inch. He got it in World War II for leading his troops out of enemy territory under cover of darkness." The class "ooh"ed and "ahh"ed. As Tyler returned to his seat, he whispered to Zack, "Try and top that!"

Everyone's head turned in Zack's direction. He knew they expected him to do something amazing. For a second he thought, "Maybe lightning will knock out the electricity and I can escape under cover of darkness."

Ms. Merkle cleared her throat. "Zachary?"

Zack coughed and went to the front of the class. His pockets held nothing but some paper clips and a tiny flashlight. "I like to stay up and read, so I use this under the covers," he said. "The beam of light is very small. It only lights about seven words. That's an area of about one square inch. So here's how I light a whole page."

Zack turned off the lights. He pointed the flashlight at a paper on the bulletin board. The lit-up area was very small.

Then Zack tipped the flashlight at an angle. "Now the light is spread out and covers a larger area," he explained. "I can angle the flashlight until the beam of light covers a whole page of a book that is 5 by 8 inches. That's an area of 40 square inches."

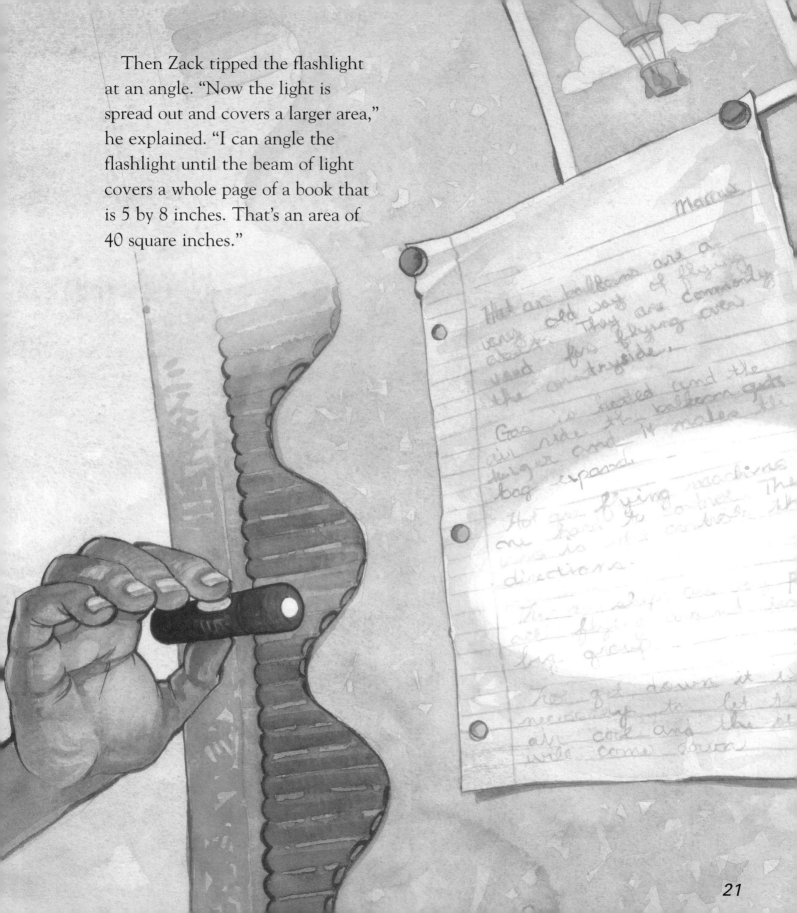

"I figured this out because sunlight on the Earth does the same thing." Zack pointed the flashlight at the globe.

"Where sunlight hits the Earth straight on, there's a lot of light and heat in that place.

"Where sunlight hits the Earth at a slant, the light spreads out and it's colder. That's one reason we have winter."

For Friday:
Bring in a rectangle and explain how you measure its area.

All the kids started talking at once. Everyone wanted to shine the flashlight on the globe. Everyone but Tyler.

The kids were so busy talking that they didn't notice when Zack turned and walked over to Tyler. There was something he had to do.

Zack took a deep breath. "Tyler?"

Tyler scowled at him. "What do you want?"

"I have to tell you a secret," said Zack.

"Yeah, what?" asked Tyler suspiciously.

"I had nothing to show today or on the other days," Zack said. "I just think things up on the spot."

He waited to see if Tyler was going to tumble out of his seat laughing or jump up and tell everyone.

"What do you mean, you had nothing to show?" Tyler said, rising from his seat.

He glared at Zack. "Then where did you get that light thing?" he demanded.

For Friday:
Bring in a rectangle and explain how you measure its area.

"I don't know," Zack shrugged. "I like transforming stuff. It's fun to change one thing into something else. And I'm always thinking of stuff I can do when I'm an astronaut."

Tyler didn't say anything for a long time.

Then, to Zack's surprise Tyler said slowly, "The light thing was really cool. I read under the covers at night, too."

"Yeah, it's the best way to read comic books," Zack agreed.

"Especially *Galaxy Warriors*," Tyler added.

"Yeah! That's my favorite!" said Zack.

"Listen," Tyler said, "can you show me how to draw one of those twisted tracks you were talking about? I just got a computer game where you can build a space station. Maybe you can come over and we can make a space track."

"A Moebius space track? Sure!" Zack said. "We can draw it like this."

The measuring assignment for next week was to draw a picture of something very big and label the height, width, length, and area. Zack knew just what he and Tyler would do. And he was certain of one other thing . . .

Friday was still his favorite day of the week.

Magnificent Moebius

To make a Moebius strip you'll need:

• a long, thin strip of paper

• tape

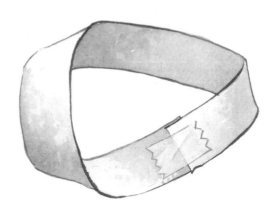

1. Twist the strip of paper one half twist.
2. Tape the ends of the paper together.
   You have a Moebius strip!

Starting from any point, you can draw
a line down the middle of the Moebius
strip. The line will end where you
started, because the Moebius strip
has only one continuous surface.

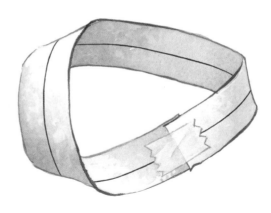

Go Further:

1. Get a pair of scissors.
2. Carefully poke a hole anywhere along the line that you drew.
3. Cut along the line. What happens?

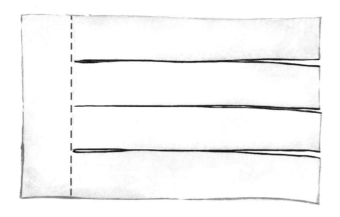

Expanding Frame

To make the frame, you'll need:
- a 4" x 6" index card or piece of paper
- a pair of scissors
- a ruler

1. Draw a line about 1" from one end (blue).

2. Cut 1" strips from the other end of the card to the line (red).

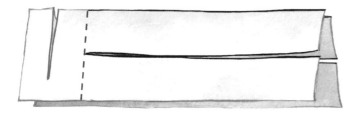

3. Fold the card in half along the middle cut (red).

4. Make a cut from the fold $1\frac{1}{2}$" toward the opposite edge (green).

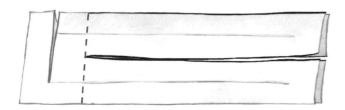

5. Starting from the green line, cut two lines (yellow). The cuts should go through both strips and stop about $\frac{1}{2}$" from the end.

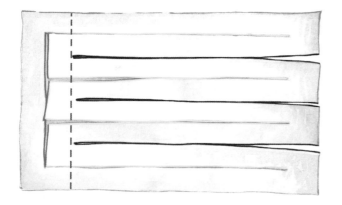

6. Unfold the card. Carefully open up all the cut edges to make the frame. Now you can step through!

The Right Light Stuff

Zack figures out how to light up a big area with a small beam of light.

You'll need:
- a small flashlight
- a ruler
- tape
- graph paper
- a pen or pencil

1. Tape the flashlight to the middle of the ruler.

2. Stand the ruler vertically on one end of the graph paper. The ruler should be straight up and down, and the flashlight should be pointing down at the graph paper.

3. Turn the flashlight on.

4. Outline the shape the light makes on the graph paper.

5. Without moving the end of the ruler on the graph paper, tilt the ruler so the light hits the paper at an angle.

6. Outline the new shape made by the light.

7. Count the graph squares in the two shapes. Which shape is bigger? Can you make a shape with an even greater area?

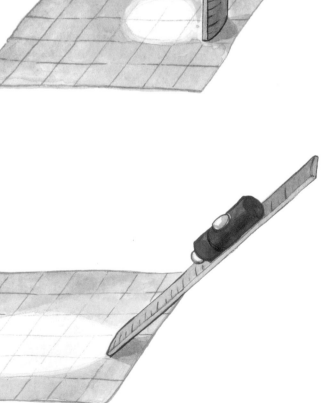